Letters to God

By
David A. Jones

PublishAmerica
Baltimore

First printing

ISBN: 1-4241-5311-5
PUBLISHED BY PUBLISHAMERICA, LLLP
www.publishamerica.com
Baltimore

Printed in the United States of America

Table of Contents

Why Is Life So Hard?

Dear God,

After so many years of witnessing and experiencing strife and pain, my over-riding question is "why is life so hard, God?" I understand the fall of Adam and Eve and its ultimate effect on our lives from that point forward. But ultimately, what is it all for? I am not entirely certain I understand how a baby born with critical birth defects or a young, innocent woman contracting cancer, suffering and ultimately dying, fits in to Your grand scheme of things. I have seen so much pain suffered by others it becomes overwhelming and, in some regards, unbearable.

I long to hear Your voice in my ear constantly assuring me that all things are for a purpose and that these events that hurt me so badly are for the greater glory of You and Your Kingdom. Unfortunately, your still small voice has been drowned out by the constant onslaught of lies screaming at me from this world.

I choose to believe that You have a purpose for everyone and everything and try in vain to put the pieces together in my mind to further assure myself of these facts; however, the deceiver continues to put so many doubts in my path. Oh, how I long to rest in the shade of Your wings and bask in Your comfort and unquestionable wisdom and boundless love.

The deceiver whispers vile questions that are designed to make me wonder about Your goodness and mercy. When I am strong, I can easily fend off these subtle assaults. However, at times like these when life has me pinned to the ground, it becomes much more difficult to ignore these lies and remain focused on You.

Love always,

Your son

Reflections on the Human Condition

Dear God,

I always find it very interesting to read Your Word, but today I find it particularly interesting to read about the sons of Abraham. My observations of current times (my lifetime) with reference to what You said regarding Ishmael and his relationship to everyone he encounters, and especially his brother Isaac, leaves me pondering not only the condition of humanity today, but also about how things would have been had Abraham not been negatively influenced by Sarah so long ago.

As I watch conditions in the East spiral ever downward, I wonder to myself how much worse things could possibly get. However, in the end I always come back to Your Promise for the answer, and then I see that things are not very different from Abraham's days. The "boys" are still at it as they have always been throughout time, and I guess they will continue that way until You call us home.

However, today I remembered Your Promise to Abraham regarding the pending birth of his son. My question to You today is, specifically what would the world be like today if Sarah had not tried to second guess You and take matters into her own hands? I cannot imagine a world without continuous strife in the Middle East that is the direct result of Sarah's disobedience to You (as if I have any room to point fingers).

The reality for me is simply that trying to second guess You never seems to work! I am somewhat envious of Abraham and so many others during that time because You spoke to them directly, removing all of the guesswork. Today, there are so many missed interpretations of Your will in our lives. I am certain that no one gets it right all of the time, and I long for the day that we can commune directly with You. However, on the other hand, those people heard from You directly and yet they still did not obey. Therefore, I have to assume that I would not be any better at obedience, though my arrogance and vanity makes me want to think otherwise.

In the end, my prayer to You remains the same: please keep me mindful of Your desires for my life and show me Your will.

Love Always,

Your (sometimes disobedient) son

Trust and Forgiveness

Dear God,

You have succeeded in teaching me a valuable lesson in trust and forgiveness. The main points that I have taken away are these:

Trust takes many different forms, ranging from the very simple and superficial types of trust that we deal with on a daily basis with virtually everyone we come in to contact with, to the very intimate types of trust that are reserved only for the closest of relationships. Finally, there is the highest form of trust, which is reserved only for You. Your Word has much to say regarding the trust that I am to have in You, yet I am left to my own devices when it comes to investing trust in others.

Then there is forgiveness; Your Word makes it quite clear that we are to forgive everyone for the wrongs visited on our lives almost daily. This remains easy to digest from an intellectual perspective, and very difficult to put in to practice.

The last few years (especially) have been an exercise in trust and forgiveness and their mutual interaction for me, and I feel that I have finally reached a point of understanding. My understanding now is that, although I am to forgive everyone for all things, trust is something that has to be earned and cannot be granted in an instant. Consequently, when someone of great trust in our lives breaches that gift, it could take a very long time (if ever) for trust to be re-established. Every breach of trust can cause great personal pain because of the damage that can potentially be inflicted, as well as the realization that we misjudged the individual and granted them a place in our lives that they apparently did not deserve.

Understanding all of that, I also realize the responsibility that I have to others as a person that has been granted trust by others. This point is probably the most sobering of the entire lesson.

Thank you, Lord, for continuing to teach me and love me regardless of my many failings in life!

Love forever,

Your son

Fatherhood

Dear God,

I have often pondered Your relationship with Jesus as Your Son and the correlation with my own children. In the earthly realms, Jesus was the personification of perfection in every way. What is He like in the Heavenly realms? Have You experienced the types of problems as a father that I face with my children? I find myself in constant turmoil over this issue. I believe that You and Jesus represent absolute perfection in every way; consequently, I cannot understand how You could have ever experienced the trials and heartaches that come from watching your children make huge mistakes and being powerless to stop them. Did You ever experience this kind of hopeless, helpless pain? On the other hand, do You experience it through my life along with every other believer? If so, how do You withstand the onslaught of such monumental pain on such an exponential level?

My prayer for today is that You teach me how to be a better parent and show me how to instruct my own children on the correct path to take through life.

Love always,

Your son

Prodigal Children

Dear God,

As I grow older, I find more correlation between Your lessons in scripture and my own life. Jesus used the parable of the prodigal son to teach me about my responsibility to my own children and forgiveness. It seems at this point that, as I find it within myself to forgive my children, I am really forgiving my own shortcomings as a parent. Whereas I do not want to be an enabler and take all responsibility away from my children for mistakes that they ultimately make in their lives, I do recognize that (at least in part) I am at fault for inadequately preparing them for the situations that they will face.

My own life has taught me that there are some things that simply cannot be passed on in the form of instruction because of the emotional element of the equation. These scenarios can be imparted as background color, showing how you ended up as the person that you are (a road map of sorts), but I don't believe that they can fully be appreciated by a third party when offered as a form of instruction. Herein seems to be the failing of the prodigal son.

I find myself in the same situation with one of my own children as the father of the prodigal son. Like him, I would have preferred that my child not go down the path that they chose, but also understand that I am (to a degree) powerless to stop them. I pray for their well-being and safekeeping, but beyond that, I can do nothing. When my child learns that what they are seeking does not really exist, I will be waiting to welcome them with open arms and forgiveness. The family unit will surround them again with love and affection and help to show them that they actually do have a place of value in this world.

The challenge that I look for guidance on is not ignoring (or under-valuing) my other children when this blessed event occurs. My thoughts on the father are that his response should have been no surprise to his other son. This should have been something that he should have prepared the rest of his family for, so that they could feel secure enough within the family to take part in the joyous event.

Father, my prayer today is in two parts: First help me to prepare my own family by helping them to understand their place in the world, and more importantly within the family. Second, help me to understand my place in Your family.

Love always,

Your son

Family Dynamics

Dear God,

Why are the interrelationships that exist within a family unit so incredibly fragile and difficult to maintain? It seems that with every person added to the family mix comes a new and unique set of complications. As if this is not difficult enough, all parties seem to interpret the situation differently, making communication about the issue almost impossible. Whereas one would assume that all parts work together for the general betterment of the whole, that does not seem to apply to family dynamics. Rather, it seems that all parts work toward their own private goals regardless of the whole! This results in an extremely stressful and dysfunctional environment for anyone who is unfortunate enough to become involved. I cannot help but think of You during the creation of man when I ponder this problem. You created our intricate bodies and managed the seemingly impossible task of making all parts work together to sustain life, and avoided the problem that I struggle with daily. How did you do that? Please give me wisdom in this area!

Jesus spread peace and love most everywhere He went in his time. However, even He, on occasion, resorted to disharmony (such as that created in the temple with the moneychangers) in order to make His point. In His particular instance though, these instances are rare (relatively speaking, given the short amount of time that He was with us).

I struggle to understand my place within the turmoil of life and look to You for guidance, direction and, most of all, understanding. Please counsel me in the art of being the spiritual leader of my family. Help me to provide guidance and instruction where needed and a firm hand only when situations require it.

Love always,

Your son

My Grandson

Dear God,

You recently blessed me with an extraordinary bittersweet event. Charles is the most beautiful baby that I have seen since the birth of my own children. When I found out about this event, I had mixed emotions. I left myself open to experience the event with no preconceived ideas, and fell in love with him almost immediately. He is so small and wonderful. It felt so good to hold him in my arms and listen to him cooing, as babies tend to do, and as much as I did not want it to happen, Charles quickly got under my skin.

I was even impressed with his adoptive parents and their families. I sympathize with their inability to have children and cannot imagine the emotion involved with waiting for thirteen years to have a baby of their own, only to find that it cannot happen. To find an expectant mother (my daughter) that is planning on adoption for her child must have seemed like an amazing blessing. This, mixed with the long anticipation of the birth and the unspoken possibility that the mother might back out at the last minute, must have been terrible for them both.

Then the blessed day arrives and everyone anxiously awaits the delivery. Adoptive parents introduce themselves to the parents of the expectant mother. Everyone gets past the awkwardness of the moment by focusing their attention on the well-being of the young woman in labor two doors down. Accolades abound for the young woman and her self-less, mature decision to give this unquestionable blessing up for adoption. All agree that this is clearly in the best interest of the child, giving her life situation. After several days of visits to the hospital and everyone extending the very best of courtesies and honoring each other's feelings and desires, the adoptive parents leave with Charles to a place of joy and happiness, while we leave with a large chasm in our lives.

As for me, Lord, I miss my grandson! I feel no shame in admitting that I am selfish in this regard. Though I am happy for the new parents, I am also envious of them, though I know what You have said about envy. That is flesh of my flesh and I feel the loss in my soul. I cannot avoid the tremendous feeling of loss in my life (one that I am very accustomed to). Please bless the life of my grandson. Set Your Angels around him and protect him from harm. Help him to grow up a good man with You in his eyes. Help him to be the person that I always wanted to be for You and failed. Most of all, please let him know how much his grandpa loves him and will miss his presence.

Love always,

Your son

Your Will for My Life

Dear God,

I have pondered on many occasions what possible will You could have for my life. Others have always assured me that You have a plan for my life, yet many of these same people say that I need to be in (and following) Your will. The problem is that I simply do not know what your will is for my life. I believe that I am saved by the grace of Jesus Christ and will see You (and all that have gone before me) in Heaven because of Your grace. I firmly believe that my salvation has absolutely nothing to do with anything that I have ever done that earns me the right to it, aside of my acceptance of Jesus (hence the free will part of the equation). The paradox for me is in the contradictory statements of others that "I need to be going about Your will for my life," but "there is no absolute way of knowing what that might be."

I have spent far too much time trying to make my will into Your will, inadvertently trying to rationalize my position into Your position, and by doing so proceeding as if things will logically work out because it is now "Your will for my life." Through the years, I have played the spiritual version of "placing a square peg in a round hole" and always to the same end. As a human, I find it very difficult to just sit back and wait for Your clarity to come over me, offering absolute assurance of the direction that I am to take. We are taught from childhood on to be "commanders of our own destiny," when we should be taught that You are the true architect of our lives and can be trusted to be our guiding light through life.

Still, as a servant, I would like to know what I should do for You. As I see this in writing, I am reminded (I assume by You) that I cannot earn Your favor or love, but that it is given freely, simply by loving You and being willing to go and do as You direct. There is no way to earn "brownie points" with You. This is a destructive function that we have patterned our entire lives after for centuries. We strive to seek favor with the powers of the time in order to improve our own quality of life, and seem to ignore the command of Jesus to "store up treasure in Heaven," viewing it as intellectual rhetoric with no real place in everyday life outside of the religious context (I guess).

In the end, I simply want to know that I am living the life that You have planned for me as best I can to Your pleasure and no one else's. I believe in You alone as a sovereign power and the One to whom I am ultimately responsible. Please guide my feet as I walk through the darkness of this life with only You to depend upon.

Love always,

Your son

Faith

Dear God,

As you know, I had a very interesting conversation with my daughter last night about faith in You. As happy as I was to have the discussion regarding this topic with her, I was even more elated to be able to voice my own position about faith. Not only did it give me an opportunity to help guide her in this very important subject, but it also served to solidify my position within myself where you are concerned.

As our conversation progressed, we discussed topics like atheism and evolution and the basic premise behind each. I explained to her that, in my opinion, these two topics (in some ways) are interrelated in such a manner, as they both require some form of physical proof for our feeble human minds to be able to grasp to. Our arrogance as humans has evolved (about the only thing that truly does) to such a level that we honestly believe that if we can find no tangible proof of a particular thing, it simply cannot be. I was very thankful for Your intervention on my behalf in providing me with clarity of thought and speech, and allowing me to explain to her that this position on the world around us was no more than our own arrogant folly and the ultimate downfall of every civilization throughout history. Inevitably, when we conclude that we can exist apart from You, some great catastrophe happens to remind us of our fragility here in the place that You created for us.

As she asked me questions about a variety of questions relating to events from history and their ultimate relevance, I explained to her that all would be answered when we are joined with You in Heaven. I was both happy and surprised (at myself) to use examples from our own extended family regarding the second coming of Jesus. This example helped me to explain that many Christians spend many pointless hours trying to form a position around when this blessed event will occur, even though Your Scripture clearly warns against this and is very clear in stating that no one knows the hour of His return. They become so engrossed in these pointless formulas that they actually make important life decisions based on these speculative dates. My point to my daughter was simply to ask the question, “How will this information enhance your life?” Quite honestly, if we knew all of these answers, what place would faith have in our lives? Faith is actually a very critical part of Your plan for us, for without faith in You what chance would we have for redemption? Thank you, Lord, for Your intervention in my child’s life, and for offering me a chance to be a witness to her. Please make these “good seeds” take root and grow in her life, allowing her to see (and focus on) You more clearly.

Love Always,

Your son

Death

Dear God,

Throughout my life, I have experienced death on many different emotional levels, ranging from mild curiosity to emotionally hemorrhaging. As a young boy in 1966, I lost my father to a cranial aneurysm, causing him to have a wreck on his way home from work one evening. I was never given the opportunity to understand and grieve the loss of my father (due to my age I assume) and only as an adult have I been able to fully come to grips with the emotional aspects contained therein.

A very short five years later death visited my home again in the form of adolescent diabetes, which struck down my older brother in a matter of two days. At the age of 11, I experienced the most frightening and horrific form of abandonment that I could imagine. My brother was my ultimate role model (actually, my only role model). In my eyes, Mark could do no wrong! He was a tall, strong, handsome young man of 14 with a great personality that everyone loved. His mannerisms were inviting and always enticed others to laughter and relaxation. Then there was me, a short, skinny, toe-headed little geek that absolutely idolized him. I spent the next thirty years trying to understand why You would take such a wonderful boy, leaving someone like me here. As I grew into a young adult, I began to experience feelings of inadequacy and resentment since You clearly took the best of my family home to be with You and left me here stripped of all of my childhood heroes.

As a young teenager, I found out that I had a little sister that succumbed to the ravages of infant influenza prior to her first birthday. My mother told me the story of how she had become very ill in the last trimester of her pregnancy with Julie and this was the result of the illness that she was born with, and ultimately the cause of her suffocation one day. Even at that early age I remember the guilt that she appeared to carry with her over those events (as if she could control it).

Through my grandparents, I learned the true depth of personal devotion between a husband and wife. I watched helplessly as my grandmother virtually killed herself trying to care for my grandfather as he was slowly torn away by Alzheimer's disease. Although she outlasted him by a couple of years, the activities of that time caused irreparable damage to her already failing heart, and eventually she passed away from heart failure.

During this time, I had been married, had two children and inherited one stepchild, learned the ultimate cruelty that can be visited on a child by their mother, engaged in the most heinous of court actions possible—divorce—and inevitably buried my estranged wife who died at her own hand. Lord, this series of events confused me more than could possibly be imagined. I could certainly rationalize the life that I had lived as having contained some invisible evil that warranted Your ultimate wrath being visited on me almost daily, but these were innocent children! Why bring them into all of this? What could I possibly have done that would result in focusing Your anger on them as well?

In time, You salvaged the remnant of my shattered life and brought me into a relationship with a wonderful woman who accepted me as I am as well as my children. In addition, You brought me a beautiful little angel named Tori who transformed my life into something meaningful. As if this was not enough, You later presented me with another daughter and I began to feel as if I was playing out the role of Job in the Old Testament. My sweet wife taught me much about You and helped me to understand many of the events of my broken past, as well as seeing all of the blessings that You had bestowed on me, and received nothing in return from me in the way of praise and adoration. Tori opened my eyes to blessings that I could have never imagined. Her sweetness and love of people was evident to all and admired by anyone who lingered long enough to fall in love with her (as they all did). I reflect with fondness even now on this wonderful time of peace in my life.

Unfortunately, peace never lasts as long as we might like for it to. Three years into this wonderful time, my mother was diagnosed with an inoperable brain tumor. This turned out to be a mix of emotions as we found ourselves resolving ancient issues from our past, and she became dependent on me as her sole source of emotional support. We talked about many things, involving my marriages and children, the places in our lives together where she over-stepped her bounds and clearly where I had under-stepped mine. I had the privilege of helping her rededicate her life to You through Jesus and was there to kiss her forehead farewell as she passed away. Though I miss the person that she became at the end, I know that in Heaven, she is free of the strife and suffering that overwhelmed her in this life.

A few years ago, I experienced the absolute decimation of my life as I knew it up to that point, when our little angel (Tori) died suddenly while away at her biological father's house for the weekend. My wife and I were broken to the very roots of our existence and faith, neither of us understanding the reason for such a travesty. This single event was the beginning of the most devastating roller coaster ride, spanning the following three years, that I have personally experienced or witnessed to date, culminating in (I believe) my wife being diagnosed with breast cancer and my eldest daughter running away from home at the age of seventeen. During this time, blessings (beyond temporal ones anyway) seemed very elusive. I struggled with virtually every facet of my life during this period, trying to understand the value of my life and certainly my value to You.

As I look back now, my past seems to equate to a common theme involving the position that things take in my life in relation to You. In most cases, the people that I lost were those that I cherished above all other things, and in retrospect, they occupied a place in my life even above You, Lord. In all cases I was afraid to put my trust where it should have been, instead preferring to lean on those people in my life. Having evaluated the evidence that my life's history has rendered thus far, and drawn the previous conclusion, I have nothing left but questions that only You can answer. Most importantly, am I ultimately responsible for the most important people in my life dying because I was too ignorant or afraid to put You above all else in my life?

Love always,

Your son

Guilt

Dear God,

Several years ago I came across a painting of a contemporary man holding a large hammer in one hand and a spike in the other. His life had completely overwhelmed him to the point of absolute exhaustion, rendering him completely incapable of continuing. In the subtle background was Jesus; fresh wounds in His hands and feet robed in white. He was prayerfully supporting the man in his decimated state and holding him close.

This image has remained emblazoned in my mind since that encounter, serving as a reminder that, primarily, I am that man! My sin prompted Jesus to avail Himself to the pain and torture that he endured on my behalf long before I was ever born. That my actions nail Him to that cross every day and no matter how much I might try or desire for things to be different, I can never measure up to the sacrifice that He made for me. Most humbling of all is the fact that, through all of this, He is always there to support me when I feel that I simply cannot go on! When life drives me into the ground, as it does on so many occasions, the only truth that I can rely on is Jesus' undying love for me.

In a world that places such incredible value on results and "self sales," it is difficult for a man to accept that no amount of work or effort or ladder climbing will ever improve his status with You, God. That the only redemption available is in the form of a man who was crucified two millennia ago as a criminal—his only crime being that He loved everyone unconditionally and strived to bring a closer walk between men and You.

Initially, this image fosters tremendous guilt in me for my part in separating myself from you. However, in the end, it gives way to peace as I become more familiar and comfortable with Your ultimate sacrifice made solely out of love for me. It also helps me to see that no amount of effort, work or pointless verbal commitment would ever be acceptable to pay You back for the distance You have gone to redeem me.

Love always,

Your son

Spousal Relationships

Dear God,

Over the years, I have had many opportunities to observe a variety of dynamics that occur between husbands and wives. These superficial dynamics have ranged from those that I consider very healthy, to those that seem very destructive. Whereas, I understand that what "seems to be" apparent on the surface is not always evidence to what is "under" the surface. What I do not understand is why people seek the type of relationships that they do.

In my past, I have suffered through a very troublesome relationship that was difficult and hard on everyone that became involved. This was a relationship born out of a "need to be needed" more than a desire to spend my life with that person. Fortunately, You redeemed my life and placed me with the person that fulfills me and makes my life complete. Now, I am at a point where I can objectively look back across both relationships (having spent equal time in both) and evaluate them for what they are (or were). I find myself occasionally looking in the mirror and asking myself "What were you thinking?!"

I have finally achieved a point of balance in my life with my wife where we function as a single unit for the benefit of both individuals, rather than so many others that we know who always operate as separate entities and are constantly in strife with one another. I have learned through this relationship that the most important factor in achieving a successful spousal relationship is having You at the center. The second most important factor is: ALWAYS place your spouse before yourself. Unfortunately, the second rule has to be observed by both partners or the results will ultimately be abusive to one partner.

I know that I am guilty of harassing men on a regular schedule by stating, "If men were perfect, they would be women." In as much as I am usually kidding, behind that statement is a tremendous amount of truth. Women (as a general rule) are much more able to maintain open communication regardless of the emotional state of affairs. In addition, women will always be willing to put others before themselves (if you don't believe me, watch a mother with her children). Women will aggressively defend their mate without question (even when they know that their partner is wrong). Men rarely display that kind of devotion and intestinal fortitude for their spouse.

Father, I thank you for the lessons that life has taught me about being a good husband to a woman who clearly deserves much better for a partner. I also ask that you keep my eyes open to lessons that I have yet to learn and especially those that I have failed.

Love always,

Your son

Women

Dear God,

What a diverse set of blessings a woman is! I have learned (with age) that, if treated with respect and tenderness, a woman can be the greatest blessing a man can have in his life. I choose to assume that this is the way You intended things to be all along. I have heard so many derogatory remarks and insulting innuendos made about women over the years. Only with age have I learned (mainly through the intensely close relationship with my wife) to appreciate the many subtle aspects of a woman.

Unfortunately, the society that I live in seems to promote one sex over the other in many different aspects rather than applauding the wondrous differences and how they accent and enhance each other. It seems that in most instances today, one has to play the fool to the other, never allowing both to maintain a level of dignity appropriate to their station.

My wife is a gift from You to be marveled and cherished. As the years pass by, I find an ever-increasing number of reasons to be thankful for her presence in my life, as well as a deeper appreciation for her wisdom and sensibility in all issues. She provides me with a wealth of reason and support when situations require me to step off into uncharted paths. When I fail at a given task or fall short of an expectation, she is there with comfort, consoling words, and reassurance, helping me to get back on my feet again and approach the situation with a fresh perspective.

Age has taught me that my wife possesses many gifts that I do not (and visa-versa), and a wise man learns to relinquish those areas over to his "partner in life," allowing her to exercise her expertise in these areas. Only when a man is able to do this does he really reach a level of maturity that fosters the growth of a truly wonderful relationship based on mutual respect and trust. In this type of relationship, neither partner is responsible for the bulk of any responsibility. Instead, they consult together and come to a consensus, which allows for mutual respect and an opportunity for all positions to thrive equally.

I have heard far too many men use Biblical prose out of context to place the man over the woman in ways that I cannot believe You intended. My intuition is that you intended men and women to be partners through life, which intimates some level of equality rather than this sex-based monarchy, which so many believe to be Your intent. As with all things, You made each with their own gifts, to be used for Your ultimate glory and not as levers against another individual.

Having spent many hours exploring this topic, I wanted to take this opportunity to thank You for my wonderful wife, and ask for Your special blessing over her throughout the coming years.

Love Always,

Your son

Marriage

Dear God,

How did things come to be such a mess with marriage partners? These days, things seem to resemble political lines in a bipartisan government rather than a partnership between two people who (supposedly) love each other. I suppose that, to a degree, we have our fast-paced lifestyle to thank for part of this mess that we have these days. On the other hand, so many people get married so early in their relationship; they hardly have an opportunity to get to know each other. Later finding out that they really have nothing in common or their core values are offensive to one another. In my case, Lord, I was so intent on being a "responsible adult" that I confused someone else's "problem" as my "responsibility" and jumped into a situation that I was completely unprepared to handle.

I guess, in many cases, divorce is justifiable (though I am not so sure that You would agree). There are so many instances of cruelty these days that I can hardly believe that you would condone that type of treatment. Did this type of behavior exist when You visited this earth in person? There is so much evil in the world today. I witness it embodying itself as mental and physical cruelty between adults that are supposed to be loving partners. I suppose that people change due to life experiences and circumstances, but I hardly believe that this warrants the emotional and physical destruction of another person.

My own experience has shown me that, with the exception of my relationship to you, my relationship with my wife is the most sacred in my life—even over that of my children. Though I love my children, those relationships will change and mature as they do. Eventually, they will go off and begin lives of their own with their partners. If I have invested everything (emotionally) in those relationships over the one with my spouse, what will I have left to me when they are gone? I have witnessed many such marriages in the past and I always wonder what the next twenty years will have for those partners when their children move on. Will they then focus their attentions where they should have been all along? Alternatively, will they find that they do not know each other—or worse, do not like each other? I find it heartbreaking that good people focus so much attention on their children and take no time out to relish the splendor of the relationship that helped spawn their children in the first place.

As for me, I am thankful for Your insight regarding my relationship, and I especially thank you for my sweet wife! She is the perfect blessing to my life and one that only a loving God could provide. I have learned a valuable lesson about waiting on Your perfect will for my life through all of the variety of relationships that I have witnessed and been part of through my years as an adult.

I love you always,

Your son

Men and Honor

Dear God,

Years ago, the majority of men were considered honorable and trustworthy. Throughout my life, I have seen just the opposite demographic illustrated. It seems that these days one must look at everyone with a suspect eye to prevent becoming a victim in some manner.

What happened to the days when honor and respect were things to be cherished by an individual? In this day and time, respect is viewed as something to be given because of station in life or position within a company, rather than something to be earned and aspired to. What happened to the idea that respect is given only to those who earn it by hard work and honesty?

Over the past fifty years, the world has seen an amazing emergence of men who are the absolute antithesis of good and honorable men. Men like Adolph Hitler who have strived for a better race of humans but who clearly did not like the human race as a whole. These men seem to drive the world to even greater depths of depravity, searching for better and faster methods of defiling the human psyche and destroying the human body. All of this in the name of "mankind" or "equality" or some other currently acceptable catch phrase that makes it more palatable to the public.

What happened to men like Moses, David, Solomon, Daniel, and Ezekiel? Men who were honorable and good in Your sight. These men respected the sanctity of Your Word and would gladly sacrifice their lives and possessions for the good of their communities. Over the past several hundred years we have seen the rise of social classism, fostering the belief that one person is better than another simply because of their station in life. This seems to be contrary to the premise that a person's worth is in the goodness of their heart and their honest desire to serve others. My culture does not provide role models like this for children to look up to. Instead, we have crooked police officers, drug-abusing athletes, celebrities that place no extended value in marriage, and of course, self-serving politicians.

I am appalled at the possibility that we have stooped to the level (as a society) that honor has become a stamp applied only to those who "can afford it." The same correlation relates to the men who founded the United States compared to those who are currently entrusted to run the country. The men responsible for documents like the Bill of Rights and the Constitution were Statesmen of the highest integrity, while the men and women of today's government are politicians; why is that? I was amazed to find that the general definitions for the two terms are vastly different as defined in a popular dictionary:

Statesman – A man who is a respected leader in national or international affairs.

Politician – A schemer who tries to gain advantage in an organization in sly or underhanded ways.

These two definitions imply completely different character traits, yet both terms are interchangeable today. I believe that the latter definition is a better overall representation of our current political structure, and I believe that there are very few in the world that can truthfully be referred to as the former.

Lord, I am truly embarrassed by the state of humanity and can only ask for Your forgiveness for our deplorable state. I pray that You open the eyes of people everywhere to the true value of honor and truth, and help lead us back to the path that You established for us.

Love always,

Your son

My Reflections on Lucifer or Satan

Dear God,

My wife and I have had many conversations regarding Lucifer (or Satan) over the years, and her perspective has helped me grow in many ways regarding my views on this unsavory topic. In many ways, this tends to be a taboo subject among our Christian peers. I am not sure if it is because they are afraid of the subject matter, or simply find it of no particular concern and therefore not worth the time to discuss openly. At any rate, I consider this a very important subject simply because, if underestimated (as many do), Satan will quietly run a muck in a very short time.

My life experience as well as my wife's has done wonders to teach me about the potential for pandemonium that Lucifer has, if ignored or underestimated. Whereas I have no particular fear of him, I do know to respect the kind of damage that he can inflict if allowed.

I choose, therefore, to acknowledge his potential ability but refuse him any power over my life, consequently allowing only You to be sole master of my heart and mind.

Society has allowed the fallen angel of light to rise to new heights of majesty in this world by sensationalizing him in movies and books. They typify him as a grotesque and disfigured creature easily recognizable and therefore avoidable, when nothing could be further from the truth. In Your Word you describe him as beautiful and cunning, a deceiver and murderer. Since I believe You, I have to believe that the fallen one is someone to avoid at all cost.

For many years, my wife has helped me to see and understand the lies and deception that Satan perpetuates throughout the world. We discuss often the condition of life in general and wonder how much longer it could possibly be before You (Jesus) return to bring this world to its conclusion and insure a world without sin, death and despair. I long to be with You, my Lord, and away from all of the daily strife that this life offers. I thank and praise You for Your grace, which allows me to live in the shadow of Your mighty wings, free from the bonds of Satan's grasp and eternal separation from You.

I Love You and Praise Your Name!

Your son

Decoding the Bible(?)

Dear God,

Lord, why are so many people so intent on finding some method of determining the future? The latest method (I am ashamed to say) is by trying to locate some hidden code within Your Word. I cannot help but believe that if they spent as much time reading Your Word as they did trying to find and decipher some hidden code, they might find that they really don't need to know what the future holds as long as they rely on You.

I always thought that it was a foolish waste of time for people to invest their lives in finding "future predictions of past events" from old documents like the quatrains of Nostradamus. All of the individuals that have focused their studies on finding out that he predicted the events of Nazi Germany have done absolutely nothing for the betterment of humanity as a whole. In the case of these documents, the language was vague enough that one could probably make the "prediction" apply to many different events in modern history; again, the major question at the end of the day being "what good does it do us?"

The current theme is to take the Bible, break it down into individual letters, and try to recognize code patterns that predict future events. This makes as much sense as taking a leaf from the nearest tree and trying to unlock the construction of the universe from it. When will people realize that if You wanted us to understand the future, You would make it clear to us? Old Testament history has provided us with countless examples of the prophets of old being granted a look at future events as You saw fit.

As for me, I am content to know that You provide me with everything that I need to sustain my life for as long as is Your will, and I need not toil with such pointless endeavors as these.

Your loving son

The Death of Our Dreams

Dear God,

It has become painfully obvious in recent years that, regardless of our desires and the fertility of our imaginations, our dreams will die, leaving us with nothing but the reality of our current existence. At first, it seems to happen with little notice on our parts, but later in life, the "deaths" seem to become much more devastating and we seem to mourn them as we would the passing of a friend or family member. Additionally, some die gently almost without notice while others seem to linger and die slowly and painfully. As with the passing of people, the passing of dreams seems to leave me with a great hollowness that is unavoidable.

Though this process can be very difficult and depressing, experience has taught me that, if I continue to look to You, I will always find something to fill that emptiness that is left. I thank You, Lord, for keeping my mind active and creative. Even though many things that I conceive never make it past the thought process, I know that You are always there supporting me and providing me with inspiration. I stand on the belief that all things (good and pure) come from You, and that as long as I draw close to You, heed Your Word, and give my life to You, I will always prevail. Though I may never achieve the grand plans that I can conceive, I will conclude this life, having completed the tasks that You have planned for me.

Your loving son through the blood of Jesus

About the Author

By the age of six, I had lost my baby sister (Julie Ann) to pneumonia, and my father (then only 36 years old) to a cranial aneurism. At that time, the prevalent school of thought was to not "burden" children with the truth about death, and, as a result, I grew up with feelings of abandonment that, at the time, I was unable to identify but were very real and would play a huge role in my life in later years. During the following five years, I grew attached to my older brother (Mark) as a key role model. I idolized him in the way that young children often do with their fathers. He was a young, strong, tall, good-looking boy with a great personality and many friends. Best of all, he protected me and cared for me as well as my older sister (Tracey). The following years were marked with watching my mother struggle as she tried to keep body and soul together for the four of us. She went through a myriad of doomed relationships and ultimately began down a path resulting in her becoming a very bitter individual. During the summer of my eleventh year, Mark developed a case of the flu (or so we thought) and two days later died from juvenile diabetes. At that point, my life (as I knew it) was in complete ruin. In an effort to cope with the life-long devastation that we had experienced to this point, we (Tracey and I) began seeking some level of "normalcy" through a variety of methods.

I began working full time at the age of 13 while still going to school, in order to provide extra income for my family. During this period, I began smoking regularly. Looking back, I am not sure if this was some sort of release, or simply because that was a normal behavior in my house. By the age of 14, I had begun my first sexual relationship that would ultimately lead me down many paths that I should have never experienced. My chosen partner (Donna) was very controlling and domineering, and by the age of 18 already had an established history of suicide attempts. By the age of 25, I had married Donna and, shortly after, she gave birth to her second child (neither of which was mine), Sarah. In 1986, my first child was born and we named her Maggie, followed by Matthew in 1988.

From approximately age 18 on, I began to sense a great need within me and looked many places for the "thing" that would satisfy this need. I experienced many different religions and found them all to be very hollow and sterile. My idea of them then was that they were filled with zombies that were simply going through the motions driven by some involuntary autonomic response to an external stimuli (I never understood it beyond that). Every path I took seemed to lead to the same dark, hollow, lonely place. In my late twenties, I began experimenting with witchcraft, sexual deviations, and marijuana. I suspect that these were all attempts to fill the gnawing void that continued to plague me with increasing intensity.

Through the course of these years, I watched Donna relapse into violent rages that came completely without warning and left her in a deep state of depression afterwards. I spent an ever-increasing number of hours at work, limiting my time at home as much as physically possible. It was also during this time that I met Kim. Kim and I became close friends, sharing the events of our lives as well as the trials of our doomed marriages. She was going through a divorce with a beautiful physically challenged child named Tori. I sensed a strength and peace in Kim that I had never seen anywhere else. Though she was faced with (what most would consider) overwhelming challenges, she persevered with a calm, quiet countenance that I truly admired. Kim minced no words in telling me how she felt about me being a practicing witch. She believed very strongly in the Lord and would allow NOTHING to interfere with that. She told me that power only came from two places, and if it was not of the Lord it was certainly from Satan, and the latter was not acceptable to her.

On one particular evening, I arrived at home and found my son crying, battered, and bruised, only to find that Donna had (once again) broken down and, during the rage, beaten my son severely. At this point, I became enraged myself, gathered my children, and took them to my mother's where we stayed for some weeks. I filed for divorce almost immediately upon the counsel of my mother (who had a wealth of experience in this area) and began a very long and difficult legal battle (or so I thought). During this time, Kim remained my steadfast friend, supporting me emotionally and always having just the right encouragement to help me keep going. She insured me that I could make it through this, and regardless of the fact that Donna insisted that I would fail without her, Kim always seemed to know that I was better than the credit I was being given. The first trial date arrived, and though I would not necessarily consider that I won, I did not lose either. My mother received temporary custody of my children (we were all living together at the time anyway), and Donna was given every other weekend and ordered to attend an evaluation of her mental state. Several days later, I received a call from Donna informing me "she was going to give me my way." I replied that it was neither in her hands nor in mine and totally up to the courts and the judge. Knowing that she was threatening another suicide attempt, I opted to call her bluff this time and not go racing to save her as I always had in the past. The following afternoon I received a call from her father, telling me that she had shot herself with the shotgun that he had provided her as a means of self-defense.

This ended the court battle and my children were "returned" to me (though they never really were out of my custody). My (then) in-laws retreated to lick their collective wounds and console themselves by levying all blame on me while my children and I began to rebuild our lives together. Time passed, Kim's divorce was long since final (though the visitation and child support would continue to be an issue for many years), and we remained close friends. We visited a local church that was of a style that Kim preferred, and I was immediately shocked by the fact that there was a BAND there! The preacher was vibrant and spoke the Word in a manner that I had never heard before. For the first time, I actually understood what he was talking about and it drew up emotions and feelings that I had never felt (at least not in church).

Kim and I eventually married and soon had our first (and only) child together whom we named Lexie. Our life together has been nothing less than amazing. My eyes were opened to so many new things that I never knew could exist. Tori filled a place in my life and my heart like nothing else ever could. Kim provided me with unconditional love and support that had been completely lacking in my life up to that point. She introduced me back to God and I found that He had been there watching after me and guiding my steps even though I denied him daily.

In May of 2002, while visiting her biological father for the weekend, Tori stopped breathing and was rushed to the hospital. Eleven emergency room doctors and nurses attended my daughter (as Kim and I watched on in horror). Tori never woke up again. At approximately 5:30 P.M. on Saturday evening, Kim did the unthinkable and went to Tori's side, kissed her gently and told her that it was okay to go and be with Jesus—shortly afterwards she died. I was allowed the opportunity (since I was a "stcp" parent, I had no right in the treatment room) to kiss my sweet daughter and say goodbye to her before leaving the hospital and beginning the horrible task of arranging our daughter's funeral. Kim and I went to church the following morning, though neither of us wanted to. Kim's reasoning was that "if we did not go then, we would probably never go again." I never could argue with her unquestionable wisdom. Time passed and we actually survived the death of our little angel (though neither of us thought we would at the time).

A very short year later at Christmas time, Kim was diagnosed with breast cancer. This announcement sent us on yet another emotional roller coaster that would span about two years and many surgeries. Kim was calm about the whole thing, resigned to whatever the end might be. Her feeling was "she knew where she was going, and if today was the day, she would be with Tori that much sooner." That was fine for her but what about me? I was absolutely terrified! The Lord had graced me with a wonderful life and a terrific wife whom I absolutely adored, and now that might all be coming to a close. I spent countless hours in the surgical waiting rooms wondering how I could possibly go on should the worst come about. In the end (of course) all was fine, but I learned what the Lord had been trying to teach me all along. I have to rely on Him only. All other things will come to an end or fail me at some point but He is always there.

Printed in the United States
64056LVS00004B/316-318

9 781424 153114